Praise for *8 Letters o*

"This little book packs a big pu

    – **Jim Lecinski**, Clini
    Northwestern University

"Fritz gives you the key rules that work to make your writing pop. No fancy talk about grammar or style — just clear tips you can use right now to make your emails, reports, and posts grab readers. Buy this book if you want your writing to stand out at work. Your boss, your colleagues, your family will all thank you."

    – **Gokul Rajaram**, Coinbase / Pinterest / Meta / Google

"Outstanding tips and tricks from the GOAT of tech copywriters! A must-read for marketers and copywriters at any stage in their career. Fritz shows time and again how to craft a message that really hits home for your audience."

    – **Michelle Wells**, VP Global Marketing, Infomedia

"Perhaps the most useful business book of the year, *8 Letters or Less* takes us on a simple journey to write with impact. A must-read for leaders and learners."

    – **Joanna Flint**, Mandarin Oriental Hotel Group / Google / Ogilvy One

"As a leader at Google, I saw firsthand how Fritz's teachings streamlined our communications. I'll be buying copies for all of my new hires."

    – **Jon Diorio**, VP Product Management, Credit Karma

"Brevity is the soul of both wit and wisdom in Fritz Holznagel's spot-on guide for why, when, and how to use short words to make an impact. *8 Letters or Less* makes a fun and lively case for using short, snappy words and punchy sentences to get your point across, simply and smartly."

– **Laura Bergheim**, CEO, Wordsmithie

"*8 Letters or Less* is a quick, fun read that will make you a better writer. Fritz weaves stories from his life in TV and tech to show how simple is always better. This book is now a required read at both my home and with my executive team."

– **Bismarck Lepe**, Founder and Executive Chairman, Wizeline

"*8 Letters or Less* isn't just helpful — it's fun! Fritz shows us how to bust through indirect corp speak and get to the point so your readers can spend time on your ideas, not decoding your phrasing. But be warned: this book will also make you want to eat tater tots, so plan ahead."

– **Ali Miller**, Instacart / Google

8 Letters or Less

Fritz Holznagel

Published by How2Conquer

Atlanta, Georgia

www.how2conquer.com

How2Conquer is an imprint of White Deer Publishing, LLC.

www.whitedeerpublishing.net

© 2025 by Fritz Holznagel

All rights reserved. No part of this publication may be reproduced, stored in a retrieval system, or transmitted in any form or by any means — for example, electronic, photocopy, recording — without the prior written permission of the publisher. The only exception is brief quotations in printed reviews.

First edition, March 2025

Ebook edition created 2025

Cover design by Telia Garner

Edited by Lauren Kelliher and Charlotte Bleau

Illustrations by Susan K. Sears

Library of Congress Cataloging-in-Publication Data is on file at the Library of Congress, Washington, DC.

Print ISBN 978-1-945783-39-5

Ebook ISBN 978-1-945783-40-1

For information about special discounts available for bulk purchases, please contact How2Conquer Special Sales at www.how2conquer.com/bulk-orders.

Contents

A Note About *You*

You're a better writer than you think.

Yes, <u>you</u>. Lots of us think (or worse, have been told) that we can't write. But in truth, if you can count to 8, use scissors, and draw a circle, you can be a very good writer — one of the best writers at your high-tech company, law firm, or tattoo parlor.

8 Letters or Less isn't like other writing guides. We won't talk about gerunds or split infinitives. We won't even talk about nouns and verbs.

Instead, we'll break writing down into a few secrets and simple tricks that come straight from a day in first grade.

You're not in first grade now, of course. You're grown up. You need help with emails, sales reports, social media posts, and work reviews. You want your good ideas to be read. These tips will help. Use them and people will enjoy what you write.

I know, because they've worked for me for 30 years. They've helped as I wrote for major clients like Google, Bank of America, and Eventbrite; for learning games like *Where In the USA Is Carmen Sandiego?*; and even as I won an Emmy as a writer of the CBS special *A Claymation Easter*.

◆ ◆ ◆

8 Letters or Less is based on workshops I began doing for Google in 2013. The head of the marketing team for Google Analytics asked me if I could, in under 2 hours, share 10 rules to help the team write more clearly. These busy people didn't want to hear about proper use of the subjunctive mood; they needed simple rules that would work in a hurry.

That first workshop went well, and soon other people began to ask me to do workshops for their teams. Over time I realized a key point: There aren't 10 vital rules, there are just 3.

Those are the 3 secrets you'll find here. They're easy rules you can start using right now, this moment, today.

If you're about to write up a new product idea, social media post, client email, press release, job listing, budget forecast, dreaded annual job review, web copy, or a plain old memo, this book is for you. If you're about to apply for a job, craft a thank-you note, or write a resume, this book is for you. And if you're about to draft a college paper, a high school book report, or a flowery love note, this book is for you, too, you crazy romantic.

◆ ◆ ◆

There's one catch: You *must* be able to count to 8 to use this book. If you qualify, let's get started!

The 3 Secrets

These 3 secrets will help you whatever your job or role: product manager or engineer, CFO or junior admin, new hire or old-timer.

They may not make you the *best* writer at your firm, but they'll move you into the *top half* of all writers at your firm. That should be enough to help you reach the next level, the C-suite[1], or wherever it is you're headed. These secrets work!

---

1 The C-suite: a group of key company jobs that begin with C (for chief). Think CEO, CFO, CMO, etc.

SECRET 1:
8 Letters or Less

Can you count to 8?

If so, you can do the one thing that will make your writing 95% better: **Use words that are 8 letters or less.**

Yes, it's that simple. You can stop reading the rest of this book right now. This is the big secret, the key to it all.

Lots of us were taught that big words are smart. That they sound *exceedingly professional* and make us look like *profoundly insightful intellectuals.* So we stuff in more words and longer words as we write, hoping that *more* plus *longer* will equal *better.*

But it doesn't work that way. Long words equal one thing only, and that's *hard to read.*

Which would you rather see in your inbox? This:

> Contemplate this transformative multitude of interminably extensive expressions, prioritized and reconceptualized in accordance with the corporate infrastructure's characteristic configurations.

Or:

> Look at these nice short words that aren't even 6 or 7 letters long. They're all so easy to scan and read. No need to stop and scratch your head here!

Bet you like the second choice better. I do, too.

Why do we like short words? It's all visual. Here's how Ferris Jabr put it in *Scientific American* (bolding mine):

> *The human brain may also perceive a text in its entirety **as a kind of physical landscape** . . . similar to the mental maps we create of terrain . . . Much as we might recall that we passed the red farmhouse near the start of a hiking trail before we started climbing uphill through the forest, we remember that we read about Mr. Darcy rebuffing Elizabeth Bennett on the bottom left corner of the left-hand page in one of the earlier chapters of Jane Austen's* Pride and Prejudice.[2]

---

2 Jabr. "The Reading Brain in the Digital Age."

Our brains see text as a landscape. And we want the view to look like this:

Nice! Smooth going ahead. We can floor it! But a sentence full of long words looks to the reader like this:

We can't floor it; we can't even go 10 miles per hour. We're gonna bust a muffler on one of those 15-letter *circumlocutions.* We'll never get to where we're going.

A few years back, the *Oxford English Dictionary* made a list of the 100 most common words in English. They're very short! If you set aside the "glue" words, like *the* and *to*, the 10 most common words are:

- time
- person
- year
- way
- day
- thing
- man
- world
- life
- hand

Not an *optimization* among them.

"Shorter and more frequent words are recognized faster . . . than longer and less frequent words," says one recent study. Short words "are processed with less cognitive effort."[3]

Simply put, long words make you work hard. And who wants to work hard? That's why long words mean less to us.

Look at the 3 groups of words on the next page.

---

3 Kuperman, Schroeder, and Gnetov, *Word length and frequency effects.*

supervisory overseer
manager
boss

augmentation
increase
raise

perambulate
proceed
walk

Which words put a picture in your head as you read them? Which hit you in the gut?

I'll guess that the last choices — the *short* choices — hit you harder. As they should. An *augmentation* is a nickel-an-hour increase, but a *raise* is a big fat deal. A *supervisory overseer* is a vague figure who might be in Estonia or even Peoria. A *boss* is someone who's peering over your shoulder right this second.

Short words look you in the eye and give it to you straight. Long words don't. Long words chew their nails and are afraid to speak their mind.

Short words work. Short words win. Short words get it done.

Hidden in Plain Sight

Warning: You'll never look at movies or music the same way after reading this next bit.

Because short words are pop culture's secret weapon. The pros don't talk about it, but their secret is right in front of us every day.

Example 1: When Rihanna sang at the Super Bowl, this was her set list of all-time hits:

- Bitch Better Have My Money
- Where Have You Been
- Only Girl (In The World)
- We Found Love
- Rude Boy
- Work
- Wild Thoughts
- Pour It Up
- All of the Lights
- Run This Town
- Umbrella
- Diamonds

See a trend? Break those hit titles down — 34 words and 141 letters — and she averages just over 4 letters a word. (4.147 letters per word, if you're a wonk.)

Now look at her lyrics:

> Want you to make me feel like I'm
>   the only girl in the world
> Like I'm the only one that you'll
>   ever love
> Like I'm the only one who knows
>   your heart
> Only girl in the world

This isn't by chance. If "Encourage you to convince me to perceptualize myself as the exclusive female internationally" is what sold records, then that's what she'd be singing.

Spoiler: It's *not* what sells records.

Grab your phone right now and Google "Billboard Hot 100"™ to see this week's top pop songs. The top 3 songs as I write this are:

- **Bar Song** (Shaboozey)
- **I Had Some Help** (Post Malone)
- **Not Like Us** (Kendrick Lamar)

Bet you see the very same kind of short words on this week's list. It's always that way, week after week. These are people whose job is to grab and hold you for 3 minutes — the length of the usual pop song. Surprise: That's *also* the amount of time your boss will spend reading your email, memo, or report. (Or that a *future* boss will spend on your resume.)

Every email you write is your next hit single. Most of the memos and reports we see at work every day are like elevator music: a flow of bland jargon we learn to ignore. To get your point across with the people who matter, you need to break through in the way a really catchy pop song does.

Short words are the beat that makes that happen.

At the Movies

What would you say is the most beloved movie series of all time? I'd say it's:

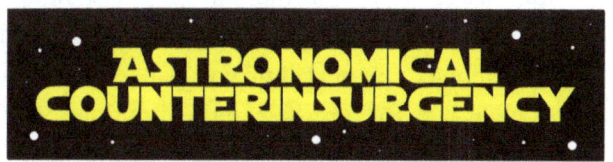

Except wait, they didn't call it that. They called it:

STAR WARS

40+ years and tens of billions of dollars later, *Star Wars* is still going strong. Look at the titles of Disney's Star Wars sequels: *Rogue One. The Last Jedi. Solo. Andor.* This is not by chance.

Sure, there's *The Mandalorian.* But who's the star that makes that show go? *Baby Yoda.* The catchphrase? "This is the way." Sounds a lot like, "May the force be with you," right? Hmm.

Maybe *Star Wars* isn't your fave film series. Maybe you'd choose one of the other giants: *James Bond. Frozen. Scream. The Fast and the Furious. Lord of the Rings. Rocky* or *Rambo. Toy Story. Top Gun. Avatar.* Even good old Chucky in *Child's Play.* See a pattern?

The Marvel films are the biggest cash cows of all time. Look at the titles: *Iron Man. Thor. Black Panther. The Hulk.*

Studio heads are big on the bottom line. Whatever puts people in seats is what they'll do. Short words make them money. The next time you walk down a long Cineplex hallway to theater 18, scan the film titles on the posters along the wall and you'll see what I mean.

Speaking of *Frozen*, Disney is known for its catchy movie songs.

Let's recall some of those hits:

- Let It Go
- We Don't Talk About Bruno
- Be Our Guest
- You've Got a Friend in Me
- How Far I'll Go
- A Whole New World
- When You Wish Upon a Star
- Supercalifragilisticexpialidocious

Okay, that last one is the exception that proves the rule. But you see what I mean.

Take it back as far as you like, to movies like *Gone with the Wind* and *The Wizard of Oz*. Take it back to Shakespeare's *King Lear* and *Hamlet* and *Romeo and Juliet*. The stuff that sticks is made of short words.

Books, Too

Quick tour of some of the great novel opening lines of all time.

"It was the best of times,
it was the worst of times."
- *A Tale of Two Cities*

"In a hole in the ground there lived a hobbit."
- *The Hobbit*

"You better not never tell nobody but God."
- *The Color Purple*

"It was a bright cold day in April,
and the clocks were striking thirteen."
- *1984*

"Mr. and Mrs. Dursley of number four,
Privet Drive, were proud to say that they were
perfectly normal, thank you very much."
- *Harry Potter and the Sorcerer's Stone*

"We were somewhere around Barstow
on the edge of the desert when the
drugs began to take hold."
- *Fear and Loathing in Las Vegas*

"Call me Ishmael."
- *Moby-Dick*

You can see what Charles Dickens, J.R.R. Tolkien, Alice Walker, George Orwell, J.K. Rowling, Hunter S. Thompson, and Herman Melville have in common: They kept it short.

They knew they had to grab you in a few words. What was true with novels then is true with emails today: It's not the most superlative and suboptimal of times, it's the best and worst of times.

To Sin or Not to Sin

Why does evil win out over good in this world? Could it be these names?

Virtue has a branding problem. *Lust* and *greed* sound fun! *Temperance* and *diligence* bore you as you're still reading them. If you ever were to fall asleep in the middle of a word, it would be *temperance*.

No wonder lust beats chastity most of the time. It's half as long!

·7·

Capital Virtues

| Humility |
| Charity |
| Kindness |
| Patience |
| Chastity |
| Temperance |
| Diligence |

·7·

Deadly Sins

| Pride |
| Greed |
| Envy |
| Wrath |
| Lust |
| Gluttony |
| Sloth |

Ads Get It

One last example: the world of ads.

A few years ago, a company called Upwave asked 3,286 Americans to name brands based just on their slogans. Here's the top 10 in Upwave's list of "most memorable" slogans. See how many you know yourself:

Finger lickin' good

Every kiss begins with ___

15 minutes could save you 15% or more

Just Do It

Snap, Crackle, Pop

You're in good hands

Taste the rainbow

Melts in your mouth, not in your hands

Maybe she's born with it. Maybe it's ___

I'm lovin' it

I see two 7-letter words there, *minutes* and *rainbow*. 5 of these slogans don't stray over 5 letters. *Just Do It*, which we'll talk more about later, is 8 letters *in total*.

The brands, by the way: KFC, Kay Jewelers, Geico, Nike, Rice Krispies, Allstate, Skittles, M&M's, Maybelline, McDonald's. How many did you know? Most of them, I'll bet.

Ad slogans have 2 jobs: to make you feel good about the brand and to make you *remember*. Ad agencies have huge budgets for this. They could buy any word in the world! Yet the words those ad budgets buy end up being 8 letters or less. As Allstate might say, that's no accident.

How to Do Short Words

So if we're sold on short words, how do we write them? Start with our golden rule:

> Use words that are 8 letters or less.

We'll shoot for words that are 4 or 5 letters long — shorter is better! — but any word up to 8 letters can stay. Any word over 8 letters goes.

Most of us can't write and count at the same time. So: *Write first, count later.* Do your normal draft, write what you want to say, then go back over it and look for those loooooong words.

When you find one, fix it with a better, shorter word. Let's say the word is *opportunity*, and the sentence is:

> We perceive an opportunity to improve our market position.

Okay. Let's pick a new word to replace the 11 letters of opportunity:

> We perceive an opening to . . .

> We perceive a chance to . . .

> We perceive a way to . . .

You choose. I like *way*, but maybe *chance* or *opening* is closer to what you mean. Fine. They're all shorter and all better.

While we're at it: *perceive* is 8 letters, right on the edge. Let's change it to *see*. That gives us:

We see a way to improve our market position.

Congrats: You just saved 13 letters and made your idea 13 times clearer.

Even words of 7 or 8 letters can often be made shorter. Take *improve* in that sentence: What about *lift*? Or what about …

We see a way to boost our market position.

I don't know about you, but that gets me a lot more juiced up than *We perceive an opportunity to improve our market position*. Now I want to know more.

Does this all seem too easy? It *is* easy, but it's not *too* easy. It just works.

How do you find good short words? I use the *OneLook Thesaurus* (onelook.com), created by my friend and former Google engineer Doug Beeferman. OneLook gives you lots of options, and it lets you sort words by length, too.

Hamburgers and Tater Tots

This is the point in my workshops where someone asks: "Can we NEVER use 9-letter words?"

Then I say, "*Certainly* you can!" :-) We all have to use long words at times. For example, the words *sentences* and *paragraphs* both get used in this book. I could say "that line of text" or "that bunch of words," but then my reader would have to guess at what I mean. Sentences and paragraphs are what they're called. No sweat.

If you're an anthropologist, you have to say *anthropology* a lot. Technical writers need to use fancy terms. At Google, the term "account optimization" was used all the time to mean "make a client's results as good as they can be." Okay. Your job may have similar words.

Let's call these *hamburger* words. When I was in first grade, we got hamburgers and tater tots for lunch on orange plastic trays. The hamburgers were fine, but the tater tots were *so good*.

Your short words are tater tots: tasty and easy to gobble! You can't stop! But every once in a while, you have to make room on the plate for a big ol' 9-letter-or-more *hamburger*. Maybe you're in *kindergarten* or you own a *labradoodle*. Maybe you want a glass of *Champagne*. Maybe you're going to *Disneyland*.

Fine! Put that hamburger word in there. Now and then. Just make sure you keep the tater tots coming. Everyone loves a dozen tater tots. No one wants a dozen hamburgers.

So often there's a shorter way. A few pages ago I wrote, "Long words chew their nails." My original line was, "Long words chew their fingernails." But on my next pass I saw that *fingernails* was an 11-letter word in the exact place I was talking about using short words. So I switched to *nails*, and you know what? It works fine. At some other time, *fingernails* might be worth it. You decide. (We could also say that long words chew their *toenails*, exactly 8 letters. But gross.)

Let's skip the toenails and talk about your company instead. What if your firm's culture insists on using certain long words like *deprecated* instead of *shut down*, or *development* instead of *growth*?

Then your question is: Are these hamburgers or just habits? Does your boss really want to read the words, "We anticipate that the project will be deprecated" at 10:30 pm, with the baby finally in bed, when she's got 20 more reports to read after yours? Or would she rather read, "We plan to shut it down"? You tell me.

And what if you DO say *shut it down* when everyone else says *deprecated*? Will it be the end of your career? Or will you sound like a person of action and a smart, outside-the-box thinker?

Most likely, people will start to tell you what clients tell me: "Gee, you have a knack for making things so clear and friendly." Lucky for me, they don't know that I'm just using shorter words. They think they're paying me for actual talent!

Some people call this "writing at a fifth-grade level," as if it dumbs things down. Don't you believe it. This is writing for real human beings and how their brains like to read. If you want to hook a reader and hold them, cheer them, teach them, and thrill them, then short words are where it starts.

The Gist

1 Use 8 letters or less.
Raise beats *augmentation*.

2 Learn from song lyrics and movie titles:
short words are the secret.

3 Write first, count later. Make a second
pass to trim back long words.

SECRET 2:
Get Rid of the Toilet Paper

What are toilet paper words? They're words with nasty bits stuck to their heels. Bits like ...

-ized

-ment

-ing

-ation

-ship

-ious

-ance

You may be Dua Lipa or Brad Pitt in Armani on the red carpet, but if you have toilet paper on your heel, then that's all people will see. Same deal with words: readers can't see your great ideas *when they're looking at the toilet paper.*

Some words have 2 or 3 pieces stuck to them — think *departmentalization.* It's like *department* raised its hand, went down the hall to the bathroom, and came back to its desk with 3 strands of toilet paper on its heel: *-al, -ize,* and *-ation.* The poor kid will never live it down.

If your email is full of 12-letter words, then that poor kid is *you.*

Lucky for us all, there's an obvious fix: Take off all the toilet paper. When you're done with your draft, grab your mental scissors and look for words with *-ized, -ation,* and all the other bits stuck to your words. Then snip those bits off.

In my first draft of this chapter I wrote:

> Some words have 2 or 3 pieces of toilet paper hanging off of them.

On my next pass, I spotted *hanging off of them* and replaced it with *stuck to them.* Now I've got a phrase that's shorter and has more punch. That's fun.

Get to the Root

How about a sentence like, "The poor relationship between our teams is causing communication issues." How do you fix a word like *relationship*?

I like to pull every segment off down to the root word. Off with -*ship*, off with -*ion*, all the way down to bedrock: *relate*. Then I redo the sentence around that root word. I may need to fiddle with things a bit to make it work:

The poor relate between ... that doesn't work. *Relate is a problem* ... won't work. *Our teams don't relate well* ... aha! That might work!

> Our teams don't relate well, so they don't communicate well.

Much better. We even get a fancy touch in there, the parallel of *relate well* and *communicate well.*

What's that? Yes, you're right! We can look for a shorter word for *communicate*. We could cut it down to "so they don't connect well," or "so they don't share data well." I like that; maybe you don't. Maybe *communicate* is a hamburger word here. You decide.

You're likely to find that when you take things down to the root this way, you also end up with simpler and stronger phrases. The straight route to your ideas becomes clearer. It's your bonus for making the key word shorter.

Ings Are Ants

One bit of toilet paper has clogged up more sentences than any other. I'm talking about -*ing*.

There's a lot wrong with -*ing*. One issue is that it makes words weaker: *run* and *jump* have a lot more kick than *running* and *jumping*. "Stand on your own two feet" has more pop than "Begin standing on your own two feet."

But the bigger problem is this: -*ings* are ants. Let one in, and the rest march after in a line, like this:

> One of our production challenges is the expense of identify**ing**, sourc**ing**, order**ing**, assembl**ing**, and shipp**ing** the necessary widgets.

See the ants? What if we got rid of all the -ings? Then we'd have:

> . . . **identify, source, order, assemble,** and **ship** the necessary widgets.

Nice! See how *ship* has so much more punch than *shipping*? The action plays in your head. What a great, blunt word to end the string with.

You can get rid of most -*ings* with a small tweak just before them. In this case, it's the phrase *the expense of* that opens the door to the ant colony.

Let's change it:

> One of our production challenges is **how much it costs to** identify, source, order, assemble, and ship the necessary widgets.

That sounds more like what a real person would say, right?

Now then: Let's *also* get rid of all the 9+ letter words: *production*, *challenges*, and *necessary*. So instead of this:

> One of our production challenges is the expense of identifying, sourcing, ordering, assembling, and shipping the necessary widgets.

We have this:

> One problem is that it costs a lot to identify, source, order, assemble, and ship the right widgets.

What a relief! We get it right away.

Side note: The same ant march happens all the time with -*ation*. As in, "We'll handle the configuration, installation, and confirmation for you," instead of, "We'll set it up, install it, and confirm it for you."

Yet one more problem with *-ing* words is this: they attract toxic friends that can really make sentences go wrong.

Let's start with a basic one: *make* vs. *making*. It's only two extra letters, so what's the big deal?

With *make*, the sentence can be simple and direct:

Let's change how we make decisions.

But when we add *-ing*, it brings along a toxic friend:

Let's change our **decision-making processes**.

Processes is the old college pal who sits on your couch and eats chips all day while you work to pay the rent. You don't need him, he adds zero to the mix, but there he is anyway.

With *-ing* and its toxic friends, even a simple sentence like ...

It's time to weed the garden.

Becomes ...

The garden-weeding should now be implemented.

If you think *processes* and *implemented* are typical business English ... they are! That's the problem. Boot these toxic couch surfers and you'll be the most readable person on your team.

Okay, YOU try it. Grab a piece of paper (or do it in your head, smarty-pants). See if you can fix these sentences. Don't be afraid to shorten other words as you cut the -*ings*.

> Once customers begin researching, reading
> reviews, viewing websites, and visiting stores,
> that's an indication they're preparing
> to purchase.

{ Go ahead, try it. We'll wait. }

How'd you do? Are you happy with it? Good. There are lots of ways to fix it. Here's one:

> As soon as shoppers start to research, read
> reviews, look at websites, and visit stores,
> they're ready to buy.

OK, here's another to fix:

> Diversifying our purchasing audience is
> an essential consideration as we begin
> transitioning to our future product iterations.

{ Your turn. }

Did you make it better? I'll bet you did. Here's one way to say it:

> We need to find more types of buyers as we move into our next group of products.

Now you sound like you know your stuff and can tell it straight. (Which you do and can, right?) Let's try one more, a resume opener:

> Experienced professional seeking to leverage extensive background in customer relationship management for Fortune 500 companies. Known for consistently driving revenue growth and surpassing goals, with a propensity for innovation.

$$\left\{ \quad \text{Can you cut it down?} \quad \right\}$$

Resumes can be tough, because we all want to sound like hot stuff. Good news: short words do that better than long ones! How about:

> Veteran customer relations expert for Fortune 500 firms, ready to put those skills to work for you. I know how to meet and beat annual sales numbers. Born to innovate.

Born to innovate. Is that too cheeky? Not to me. It's what we really mean, isn't it? *Innovate* has so much more power than *for innovation.* When your words have punch, *you* have punch.

Try It Yourself

Okay, end-of-chapter quiz. Grab the last thing you wrote for work — an email, a report, an update — you choose.

Go through the first big paragraph and fix any word over 8 letters. Get rid of all the *-ings* you can. Cut every toilet paper word, even if it makes things sound awkward. Be ruthless.

> While you're doing that, I'll take
> questions from the audience.

What if I just can't find a shorter word?

See **The Big Flip** on **page 71**. You can fix the sentence instead of the word. Next question, please.

Can we NEVER use -ing?

Sure we can. Even Google put *I'm Feeling Lucky* on its home page in 1998. They seem to have done okay. Every now and then, *-ing* works fine and makes things easier to read.

Take a phrase like,

> I was texting a friend when the unicorn flew into my room.

There are ways you *could* work around that:

> I had just sat down to send a text to a
> friend when . . .

or:

> I was about to reply to a text from a
> friend when . . .

But those phrases don't mean quite the same thing, and they aren't simpler, either. "Texting" is a common term. Keep it!

Or maybe you want to go rock climbing. You could tell your friends, "I go now to climb rocks," which is great if you want to sound like Julius Caesar in cargo shorts. But more likely you will say, "Wanna go rock climbing?" Everyone knows the term. The *-ing* is not the end of the world.

Think of toilet paper words like hamburger words: let them do their thing in the rare moments when they work well. Then cut them everywhere else.

$$\left\{ \quad \text{End of questions.} \quad \right\}$$

Okay, how did your rewrite work out? Did you cut the *-ings*? Bet your text got shorter and sharper. Bet it hits harder. It's easy when you get rid of the toilet paper.

The Gist

1 Pull off *-ized*, *-ment*, *-ation* and other added toilet paper.

2 To power up your words, get rid of *-ing*.

3 To fix, go down to the root word and rewrite the sentence.

SECRET 3:
Serve the Steak First

Serve the steak first means: put your big message right up front.

It sounds simple, so why don't we all do that already? Because we've been trained from birth *not* to do it. For example, look at the menu on the next page.

This menu could be from any cafe in America. We all know how a menu goes:

- First, the small stuff (olives, garlic bread)
- Next, soups and salads (the kale Caesar)
- Then, slightly bigger stuff (turkey melt, BLT)

And finally, at last, at the end, the thing we've built up to:

- The ENTRÉES (New York Strip, baby!)

～MENU～

APPETIZERS

Assorted Olives	$6
House Pickles	$5
Soft Pretzel *With Bavarian mustard*	$9
Garlic Bread	$6
Hummus Platter *Olives, peppers, pita bread*	$11

SOUPS & SALADS

Garden Salad	$12
Spinach Salad *With strawberries and mint*	$9
Chicken Cobb	$10
Kale Caesar	$8
Thai Noodle Salad	$11
Soup du Jour	$5
Cup of Chili	$5
Clam Chowder	$6

SANDWICHES

Turkey Melt	$12
Grilled Cheese *Add soup for $3*	$9
Nan's Veggie	$8
Italian Stallion	$11
Reuben	$12
Tofu Tacos	$10
Tuna Salad	$9
Cheeseburger & Fries	$10
BLT	$9

ENTRÉES

Grilled Wild Salmon *Soy-ginger dressing, mashed potatoes*	$26
Chicken Pot Pie	$18
Fish & Chips *Halibut or cod*	$21
Fettuccine Pesto	$16
New York Strip Steak *Our house special! With mashed* *potatoes and asparagus*	$40

On a menu, the big stuff comes last.

We do the same thing at home. When *you* have friends over for dinner, do you start with the lasagna? No. Bet you start with cheese and crackers. As a kid, I knew that company was on its way when mom brought out that special glass dish for sweet pickles, black olives, and carrot sticks.

What does food have to do with words? Most of us *write* like we *eat*. We start with the olives and pickles. We give the reader little carrot sticks to nibble. If we work for a company called Generic Co., the olives and pickles might look like this:

> Here at Generic, we are always proud to innovate. It's part of our DNA to create fresh ideas and help our users find new ways to do things. And sometimes, those innovations can take exciting new forms. That's why today we are very pleased to announce a new type of beach footwear called Atomic Flip-Flops.

"We are always proud to innovate," that's a nice thought. What could be wrong with that?

What's wrong is that it's tooooo sloooow. People tune out before they get to the fourth word. To grab today's reader, you've got to get to the sizzling steak in the very first sentence.

Like this:

> Atomic Flip-Flops are here. This new sandal
> from Generic Co. uses advanced Sand Tech™ to
> give you the best beach trip you've ever had.

Now you can talk about Generic's proud creative DNA and whatnot if you like. But you probably won't want to, because who needs the olives and pickles once the steak is on the table?

What do pickles and olives look like? Here are some classics:

> "In today's increasingly mobile environment,
> where we carry our smartphones with us
> everywhere and have our earbuds in at all times,
> it can be hard to . . ."

> "Whether you're in retail, hospitality, or the
> service industry, there has never been a more
> amazing time to . . ."

> "Have you ever wondered where great ideas
> come from? Have you ever stopped to think
> about how Albert Einstein had that very first
> 'eureka' moment when he created his theory of
> relativity? Well, have we got an idea for you . . ."

This kind of thing can go on for pages — while the reader nods off. You've got to cut it.

Think of your boss as a wild animal — a hyena, maybe — who wants to grab the biggest hunk of meat, dash away with it to their den, and gnaw on it. A hyena does not want your pickles and olives! Your job is to dangle your juiciest hunk of meat at the start of your report, where your boss can snatch it with ease.

In that spirit, **page 46** shows what your writing 'menu' should really look like.

What happens if we write it this way? People see the steak right away, first of all. They can't miss it. So a lot more people will *order* that steak.

Note to vegetarians: Sorry for all the meat jargon in this book! Feel free to adjust as you like: use *grapefruit words* instead of *hamburger words* and serve the *pasta* first. (But please, keep the tater tots).

~Menu~

NEW YORK STRIP STEAK

This is it!
Hot and juicy, with mashed potatoes

$40

APPETIZERS

Olives	$6
House Pickles	$5
Soft Pretzel	$9
With Bavarian mustard	
Garlic Bread	$6
Hummus Platter	$11
Olives, peppers, pita bread	

SOUPS & SALADS

Garden Salad	$12
Spinach Salad	$9
With strawberries and mint	
Chicken Cobb	$10
Kale Caesar	$8
Thai Noodle Salad	$11
Soup du Jour	$5
Cup of Chili	$5
Clam Chowder	$6

SANDWICHES

Turkey Melt	$12
Grilled Cheese	$9
Add soup for $3	
Nan's Veggie	$8
Italian Stallion	$11
Reuben	$12
Tofu Tacos	$10
Tuna Salad	$9
Cheeseburger & Fries	$10
BLT	$9

ENTRÉES

Grilled Wild Salmon	$26
Soy-ginger dressing, mashed potatoes	
Chicken Pot Pie	$18
Fish & Chips	$21
Halibut or cod	
Fettuccine Pesto	$16

Now, there *is* a menu where the good stuff does come first in exactly this way: the kids menu. There's no boring house salad on the kids menu. They get right to the hits: hot dog, grilled cheese, chicken fingers. That's where you want to be with your text: steak and chicken fingers first.

In the case of Generic Co. and their flip-flops, here's how a steak-first write-up might look:

> Say hello to **Atomic Flip-Flops**, the new beach shoes from Generic. Atomic Flip-Flops are something new in footwear: They lift and separate your toes and bring you relief from . . .

Etc., etc. You can write the rest of this yourself. But you'll admit that after that first sentence, there's no doubt about the purpose of this press release. Maybe you want to read more; maybe you don't. Maybe you hate flip-flops; they make your toes look fat. But you *do* know exactly what the product is.

The writing team at Google has a term for this idea: *ruin the ending.* News writers have a weirder term that you may also have heard: *the inverted pyramid.*

In a news story, the steak comes first:

> A bus plunged off a road in Yellowstone National Park today, killing 23.

The Inverted (Food) Pyramid

Then come the soup, potatoes, olives, and pickles: where the bus was from, who was on it (a tour group on their way to a casino, always), if the roads were wet from rain, and all the rest. The more room you have, the more pickles you get.

If we wrote a bus plunge story the way most of us write corporate memos, it would look like this:

> Have you ever wondered how buses get around those tight corners in the Rocky Mountains? Many people have concerns about bus safety, and in fact many passengers avoid riding buses in the mountains due to their safety concerns.
>
> Here at *The Daily Bugle*, we are always on alert for stories about buses and national parks. For just this reason, we often assign reporters to cover those kinds of stories.
>
> That's why we are now in a position to tell you that, just as we were concerned about, a bus full of tourists plunged off a road in Yellowstone National Park this morning, killing 23 people.

You see the issue. It's slow.

It's not that details don't matter. They do! Many people who read your memo will want to know the who, how, why, and more. But the steak has to come first.

Start with the Sizzle

None of this means your steak has to be bare and boring:

> Here's a report on footwear.

Have you ever heard the sizzle of a platter before the server actually showed up with the steak? You can do the same thing with your first sentence. For instance:

> **89%** of Americans say they've lost a flip-flop in the last year.

Numbers always sizzle. With that big number we see right away *why* a new kind of flip-flop is needed, maybe with a surfer-type Velcro leash for the ankle.

Other details can sizzle in the same way:

> Flip-flops became a surprise fashion hit after Beyonce[4] wore them onstage at Coachella.

Nice! Now we want to know more. But here's the thing: The very next item after the sizzle had better be the steak being set down by the server. (That's you!)

> **Sizzle: 89%** of Americans say they've lost a flip-flop in the past year.

> **Steak:** Today, Generic brings you the solution to that problem: **Atomic Flip-Flops**, with an ID chip built in.

---

4 A made-up example. Beyonce does not, as far as we know, endorse flip-flops.

Or however it goes. (The ID chip idea may be better than the leash, TBH.)

Here's another great example of sizzle plus steak, in a news story by Ian Austin of *The New York Times*:

> *"OTTAWA — For decades, a job at Labatt, one of Canada's two major breweries, came with an unusual perk: free beer for life. But now, the company's retirees have been cut off.*
> *In a memo to employees, the brewer, which is owned by the beer giant Anheuser-Busch InBev, said it would gradually turn off the retirees' beer tap over the next two years."*

This story could have started more bluntly: "Labatt has decided to end a free beer program for its employees." Then it would go on, "People used to get free beer for life if they worked at Labatt for a certain amount of years," and so on.

But instead, the writer grabs you with "OMG, Labatt workers used to get free beer for life!" Then we get the steak: Now they've been cut off.

A quote can be steak! Here's a typical sales report an ad agency staffer might send up to their boss:

> Asako and I went to Utica for a meeting with Jan Brown, Vice President of Sales at Generic Co. We talked about how Generic wants to find better ways to reach its core audience of bearded young rock climbers. They're very interested in increasing their spending on video ads on TikTok and other social media platforms. Jan told us, "We will find the budget for smart ideas."

This isn't awful. The sentences are clear and direct. But for this reader — the boss who is dying for a sale — is that really the steak, that people went to Utica? No! The steak is right there in the last sentence:

> "We will find the budget for smart ideas."

That's big news! These people are ready to spend. So let's put it up front:

> **"We will find the budget for smart ideas."** That was the message from Jan Brown, Generic Co. VP of Sales, after a discussion with Steve and Kim of our sales team. Generic wants to find better ways to reach its core audience of bearded young rock climbers who (etc., etc.).

That's a hunk of steak that will delight any boss's inner hyena. Now let's make it even juicier for them.

Where to Find the Steak

It takes some practice to spot your steak. Here are 3 ways to look for it.

1. **If you have big news,** that's the steak.

If you're doing a press release, just ask yourself: Why is this release going out now? If you're doing a sales report for your boss, the steak could be one of several things. Did you make one very big sale? That's probably it. Did your overall sales go up 23% from last quarter? That number is your steak. Did a client ask for a meeting before making any more decisions? That may be the steak. What's the one thing your boss, or any reader, should know?

2. **If you don't have news,** then the steak is likely to be **the benefit to the reader.**

Let's say you're writing website copy for a classic feature of your software platform. It's not new, so that's not news. The feature hasn't changed either, so that's not news. It's just a good thing that exists. So what's the headline, "Feature exists"? Ugh.

Try the benefit for your reader instead:

> Save money with [our gadget].
>
> Track your project hours better with [our gadget].
>
> Help your team work together with [our gadget].

This is where numbers can be juicy steak. Maybe you found out that 82% of users say they get more done with your product. Good!

> 82% of users say teamwork is better with [our gadget].

If teamwork is an issue for me, that number will grab me. The benefit is clear. Then in the next few sentences you take me deeper into all the product's great details.

3. **What happens next?** If you don't have news or a benefit, look for **the idea that inspires action**.

"We went to Utica to meet a client" is a key fact, but it won't lead a reader to think, "So then let's do X." But if you hear that a client will find the budget for smart ideas? Now we know what will happen next. Your boss will say, "Let's give them those smart ideas!

All of these are roads to the same end: serve the steak first. Give your hyena the meat right up front. They'll see the good work you've done, and they'll read on for more.

The Gist

1   Dump the olives and pickles!
Serve the steak first.

2   Start with the sizzle, your juiciest bit.

3   Numbers make great steak.

6 Tricks from an Old Pro

Raymond Chandler, great author of crime novels such as *The Big Sleep* and *The Long Goodbye*, had a good line about the arc of a writer's life. He said at first the writer is full of gusto but knows none of the tricks of the writing trade. By the end of the writer's career, Chandler said, "He knows all the tricks and has nothing to say."

In this section, you'll find 6 of those crucial tricks of the trade that I've learned over the past 30 years. (I still have more to say, it turns out.) These are things I use daily in my life as a writer for hire. They're money-makers for me. You may not need them every day, but they sure come in handy when you do.

TRICK 1:
Check Your
First Word

Did you just finish a lengthy email or a report? Great job! Now go back and look at the first word of the whole thing. That's right: the very first word in the very first line.

Hot tip: That word should not be "I." As in:

> I think that we can solve all our problems by making better widgets.

Your reader wants to hear about *them* and what *they* need, not about you. That's human nature. So if you're writing an email for your team, the better way to put it is:

> Our team can solve all its problems by making better widgets, I think.

There are other ways to tackle this, like maybe you put the widgets first:

> Better widgets — that's the answer to our problem.

The key thing is that it's not about *I, I, I.*

In the same way, if you're writing on behalf of Generic Co., your first words also should not be "Generic Co." or "Here at Generic Co." Let's say we're writing a blog post. Here's one typical way to begin:

> Generic Co. is pleased to announce a new partnership with Big Corp.

But the real news is that Big Corp. has joined us as our partner. So let's give them the first word:

> Big Corp. has signed on as Generic Co.'s newest partner, we're happy to announce.

Our new friends at Big Corp. will be glad to see that we've put them first. Readers will get the message faster. And everyone will get a more subtle message: We don't think it's all about Generic Co.

When you change your very first word to be about the reader instead of you, you'll notice that phrases get simpler and better, almost like magic.

> **Original:** Generic gives your business the ability to grow quickly.

> **Rewrite:** Your business grows faster with Generic.

It also tends to bring the benefit to the surface:

> **Original:** Generic has just added a new two-step verification program to your account.

> **Rewrite:** Your account is now safer from hackers, thanks to Generic's new two-step verification program.

A rule of thumb at Google has always been: Google isn't the hero, the *user* is the hero. Google doesn't do stuff; Google helps *users* do stuff. That's why the home page looks like this:

No news, no ads, no blather: Just a search box that asks the user what's on *their* mind. "I need to know this." "I want to do that." If you can make your very first word serve the same purpose, then you'll be way ahead of the game.

Now, you might want to break this rule at other places in your email or report. Maybe you want to write, "I know that some people say . . ." or, "I went to the help desk and learned . . ." You'll find some examples of that in this very book. Don't sweat it. Not the end of the world.

Just don't make it the very first word of the whole thing. Don't start with *I* — start with *them*.

TRICK 2:
The Hero Word Goes First or Last

If you have a hero word — the key to your thoughts, the vital idea, the can't-miss term — it'll work best at the very start or very end of the sentence.

Let's say you've been asked to speak to the National Dairy Council about the state of cheddar cheese in America. Two good ways to start your talk are:

> Thank you for asking me here to talk about **cheddar cheese**.

> **Cheddar cheese** is why we're all here today, so let's get fired up!

A not-so-good way to start would be:

> I'm here today because **cheddar cheese** is a topic of much interest.

If the hero word is at the front, it catches the reader's eye as the first thing they see. If it's at the end, it lingers in their mind like the ring of a gong. But if the hero word is lost in the middle, the whole sentence gets lost. The reader has to work to find the key idea.

Random question: Do I have to think of *cheddar cheese* as one 13-letter word because it's all one concept? What about words with hyphens, like *13-letter* or *sister-in-law*?

Answer: You're good! Space between words is what counts. A hyphen looks like a space because it gives us room to breathe. So *cheddar cheese* is a 7-letter and 6-letter word, and *sister-in-law* is 3 words of 6, 2, and 3 letters. Spaces to the rescue!

Another example:

> Gold widgets have become our best-selling product. *(Yes!)*

> Our #1 product is now — surprise! — gold
> widgets. *(Great!)*

> We now sell more gold widgets than anything
> else in our lineup. *(No!)*

Gold widgets are amazing, so don't hide them in the weeds of the sentence. Put 'em where they can stand out.

The end spot is doubly good if your hero word is short and punchy. Let's say you want to write about how you love to shop for bargains. You could say:

> When on vacation, I love to look for bargain
> goods in thrift store shopping sprees.

But why not say:

> When on vacation, I love to look through thrift
> stores for junk.

Nice! A punchy word like *junk* lands like a hammer back there. The reader feels that, takes a breath, and plunges on into the next sentence.

Think of your hero word as the engine that moves your railway train: It should be (mostly) at the front or (now and then) at the end.

TRICK 3:
Numbers Go First

Numbers tell a whole story in one or two digits. Any number in a sentence is sure to be the hero. So put numbers first every chance you get.

Here's how it looks when numbers get lost in the weeds:

> According to a survey of 35- to 54-year-old Hispanic males done by Generic Research in January of this year, a total of 78% said they had a smartphone.

Feel that? Now look what happens when the number goes first:

> **78%** of Hispanic men aged 35 to 54 have a smartphone, according to a Generic Research survey done in January.

Once we put **78%** at the start, good things happen. Like, the number and the subject (Hispanic men) can suddenly go hand-in-hand, instead of being separated by a heap of words.

If your boss the hyena skims the report for meat, they'll get the point of this section in the first 10 words. They can skip the details if they like (who did the study, how and when it was done, etc.) because they're already gnawing on that juicy grass-fed number.

Once the number is up front, don't be afraid to boost it visually, too:

> **98%** of men say they prefer sushi to nachos.

Bold it or make it bigger. Turn it red or green if you like. Go nuts. It's your report — do what you need to get it read.

Here's an added secret: Active numbers are stronger.

Compare:

> 98% of men **said** they preferred sushi to nachos.

To...

> 98% of men **say** they prefer sushi to nachos.

Which one is juicier? Which one sounds like you should act on it today?

If a thing is here and now — men *prefer* sushi — it's more urgent. You can act on it. So write your numbers as if they're in play right now.

Bonus points if you noted that we could cut "say they" and just write, **"98% of men prefer sushi to nachos."** In this case I happen to like the visual action of all these men *saying* it. But you do you.

TRICK 4:
Try the Big Flip

What do you do with a sentence that you just can't fix? Maybe the words are long and awkward. You can't find a way to cut off -*ing*, or to get it right. You're stumped.

Here's the trick I use in those cases: Cut the sentence in half and flip the two parts, putting the halves in reverse order. Then rewrite from there.

Say you're not quite happy with this sentence:

> Generic enables your new business to grow more quickly.

Let's cut it in half. You can eyeball it, or if you're neurotic like me, you can count to the exact middle, 27 out of 54 letters and spaces.

When I get there, I make my cut and flip the parts:

> siness to grow more quickly. Generic enables
> your new bu

Okay, that's dumb, let's keep the full words together. That gives us:

> business to grow more quickly. Generic enables
> your new

Aha! Now we get a whole new idea for this sentence. Instead of the focus on Generic enables, we focus on the business and its growth. Let's take those jumbled words and use them to make a complete sentence:

> Your new business grows more quickly when
> enabled by Generic.

If I like that better (and I do), then I can tweak and trim even more:

> Your new business grows more quickly with
> help from Generic.
>
> Your new business grows faster with help
> from Generic.
>
> Your new business grows faster with Generic.

Maybe even ...

> You'll grow faster with Generic.

That's about as short as I can figure out how to get it.

While we're at it, we've also flipped the focus onto the client and their business, just like we did a few moments ago in **Trick 1** when we changed the very first words of the press release from "Generic is pleased" to "Big Corp. has signed on." That's always a good idea.

Now *you* try to fix this bit of promo copy:

> The Generic Organization impacts music education through our ongoing work in training teachers, funding concert halls, and inspiring students of all ages.

{ A pause as you work through this... }

Okay, what have you got?

Here's how I'd do it. First, the flip: The halfway mark comes right about after "work." So:

> in training teachers, funding concert halls, and inspiring students of all ages. The Generic Organization impacts music education through our ongoing work

That's a pretty neat break. The simple flip would be:

> Training teachers, funding concert halls, and inspiring students of all ages is how our organization impacts music education through our ongoing work.

Not bad. But let's get rid of all those *-ings* ...

> Train teachers, fund concert halls, and inspire
> students of all ages — that's how our organiza-
> tion impacts music education through our
> ongoing work.

It's a bit awkward, but we can fix that with a few more tweaks and trims:

> We train teachers, fund concert halls, and
> inspire students as part of our ongoing work
> to boost music education.

It's a bit of a cheat to change "Generic Organization" to "we," yes. Maybe we can't do that if this is the start of a press release. But that caveat aside, I like this version better. The action is up front, and every word is 8 letters or less up to *education*. Not bad at all.

After you make a change like this, put the original line side by side with the new version. Read them aloud if you like. Which is clearer? Which would you rather read yourself?

The Big Flip works because it jolts the sentence like a shake of Boggle cubes. Even if the flipped version doesn't quite work, it'll give you a fresh way to think about what you really want to say.

TRICK 5:
Yes, You Should Cut That

Years ago, when I was a newbie in the film and TV business in Portland, Oregon, I worked at times as a gofer for the ad agency Wieden+Kennedy. They went on to do landmark ads for brands like ESPN, Old Spice, and KFC. Back then, their big client was the shoe company Nike.

One day I went to a pre-shoot meeting in the office of co-founder Dan Wieden, and on a white board on his wall, in block caps, were these words:

JUST GET OFF YOUR ASS AND DO IT

At the time I figured it was just advice to himself. And good advice it is! No word longer than 4 letters. It's catchy, edgy, and direct.

One year later I saw a swell TV ad with Nike's new slogan, which (as you know) was *not* JUST GET OFF YOUR ASS AND DO IT. The slogan was:

JUST DO IT

Wow. 5 of the original 8 words on that white board got cut. Does it work? You bet! The longer version *might* have worked, but the shorter version clearly *is* a huge hit. Nike still uses it, decades later. (It fits on a shoe box, too.)

Nike's slogan could have been, "Please exhort yourself to get outside and exercise. It's good for you, and you'll find it has many benefits." But instead, they turned it into an order, an urge, a heroic command: JUST DO IT.

Could Wieden+Kennedy have cut further? Could the phrase have been DO IT?

Or even just: DO?

Sure. Would it have been as popular? Who knows? The point is: If W+K could cut 62% of their original slogan, you can cut 20% of your words (or more) without losing much.[5]

---

5   In later years, Dan Weiden said the phrase was inspired by "Let's do it," the words of criminal Gary Gilmore before he was shot by a firing squad in 1977. Maybe so! I saw what I saw.

When you cut words, you make things better. You distill. You go from a barrel of corn to a bottle of bourbon. You trim the fluff off the poodle.

Old-timey author W. Somerset Maugham put it this way, according to writer Paddy Chayefsky:

"If it should occur to you to cut, do so."

Maugham is a trivia question now, but he was a huge star of the 1900s with novels like *Of Human Bondage* and *The Razor's Edge*. He could really write!

His point with that quote was this: If you look at a word or paragraph and think, "Should I cut this part?" or, "Do I really need this?", then you've already answered your own question. Cut it. If it was a must-keep, you would never have asked. And if it's not a must-keep, it has to go.

The natural human urge, when you're unsure, is to *just in case* stuff. "Oh, I'll leave that 4-day-old pizza slice in the fridge *just in case* I want it tomorrow." "Oh, let's put that old coffee table down in the basement *just in case* we need it."

> **Pro tip:** You will not want the 4-day-old slice of pizza or the coffee table, and neither will your reader. They don't want your *just in cases*. They only want your *musts*.

So you've got to Marie Kondo your sentences. Any idea that doesn't "spark joy" has to go.

This rule is a comfort to me because it makes life easy. Question to myself: "Gee, I'm not sure. Does this belong?" Answer: "Cut it." I cut words, cut lines, cut whole sections. They might be very good words! But if they aren't musts, then they have to go.

Make those cuts and you'll see for yourself that this rule works, because the next time you look at your piece, you won't recall what you cut out. What seemed like a *must* on the first pass was . . . not a must. In decades of writing, I've regretted a cut maybe once or twice but been glad hundreds of times.

If people want more, they can always ask for it. (Bet they won't ask.)

You may find cuts painful at first. Even surgeons get queasy the first time they cut into a real body. But they get used to it, and you will, too. Think of yourself as a word surgeon: You save the patient by taking out the appendix. What's it for? Is it useful? Maybe, but probably not. Better to cut it out.

Just do it.

Trick 6:
Respect the
Circle of Steak

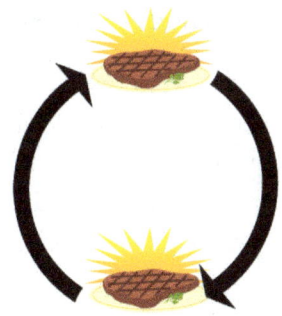

Can you be a better writer just by drawing a circle? Yes!

If you've seen *The Lion King*, you know the song "The Circle of Life." All the animals of the jungle come and bow down to their future king, baby Simba. Who will later hunt and eat many of them. (He's a lion!)

Let's not dwell on that part. The key point is: It feels good when life comes back to where it starts.

This can be a powerful trick when you write. The trick is called: *The Circle of Steak*. You serve the steak at the start of your piece, then *circle back* to the steak at the very end. Your original point is driven home again (good!) and the reader gets a warm feeling of closure.

Let's say you work for Generic Co., the flip-flop makers, and you begin a proposal to your boss with this stunning (and quite tasty) bit of steak:

> 63% of Americans call them **shower shoes**, not **flip-flops**.[6]

Great start! Then you go on to talk about how Generic should get rid of the name *flip-flops* and call them *shower shoes* instead, or measure social media posts for name trends, or run ads that say *Shower Shoes Are Old News*, or whatever swell idea you have.

You state your case for 400 words, and you come to the end. Now you're stumped — how to wrap up? Do you say, "Thanks for reading"? Or, "That's all"? Or, "We should also make fake Crocs, I'll talk about that in another memo"?

No! You, genius you, use the Circle of Steak. You remember that your first line was, "63% of Americans call them *shower shoes*, not *flip-flops*." So now you circle back to it with a line like this:

---

6 This number is made up! Please do not base your next start-up on it.

> You say flip-flops, I say shower shoes, but we all want to sell more of them.

Or:

> This name change may not be easy, but 63% of Americans will thank us.

Or:

> Let's make sure that a year from now, every American says **flip-flops** first.

You see the point. You take your last line and plug it back into the first. It's like the Indy 500: You cross the finish line at the same place you started.

I know, I know: It's so simple. It hardly even feels like a trick, right?

Spoiler: If you skip to **page 90**, you'll see me pull this trick on *you*.

But if you *don't* end with a circle back, then it feels like you wandered off. You told the reader you would bring them bagels, you went out, you stopped for a coffee, began to chat up the cute barista, forgot the food, and came back empty-handed. Not good. The reader *wants* you to bring back those bagels.

The circle of steak doesn't even have to be clever. If you can make it smart and snappy, that's great.

But if it's just a near-recap of the first line, that's *also* great. Just be sure you close the circle and take the reader's mind back to where they started.

"Okay," you might say, "What if my piece is only two sentences long? What if it's a social media post?" Point taken, smarty. But even on social media, you can and should use the circle in long posts or threads. Example:

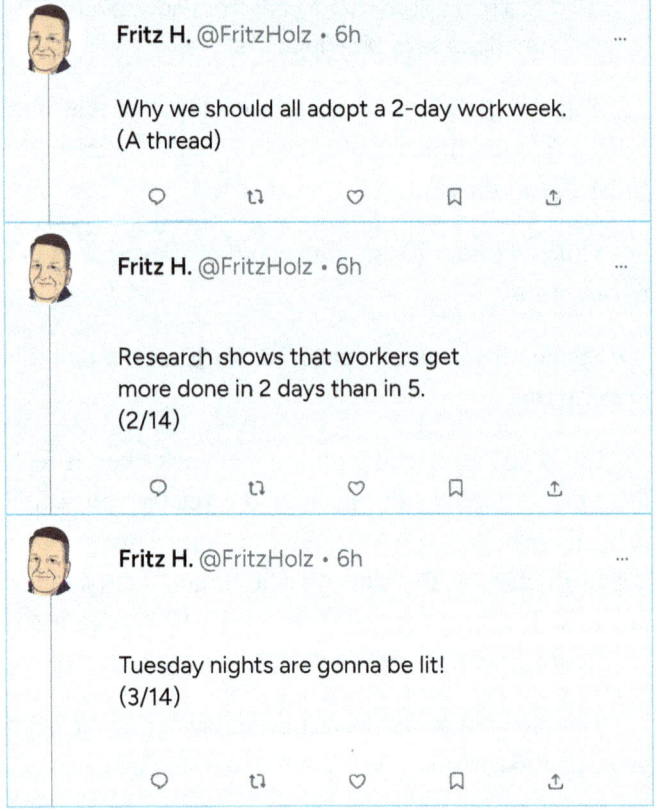

Fritz H. @FritzHolz • 6h ···

Why we should all adopt a 2-day workweek.
(A thread)

Fritz H. @FritzHolz • 6h ···

Research shows that workers get
more done in 2 days than in 5.
(2/14)

Fritz H. @FritzHolz • 6h ···

Tuesday nights are gonna be lit!
(3/14)

[And so on.]

Now we've come to your 14th and final post. We *could* end it with the last item on your list:

Fritz H.
@FritzHolz
...

Less wear and tear on office chairs. (14/14)

3:32PM • March 11, 2025 • **245K** Views

But that ending leaves me feeling lost. Is that it? Are we even done?

To feel good about it, we need to circle back to where we started. We can make the circle simple and direct:

Fritz H.
@FritzHolz
...

And that's why we should all adopt a 2-day workweek. (14/14)

3:32PM • March 11, 2025 • **245K** Views

It can be fancier:

It can include a very specific call to action:

You'll find many ways to circle back to the steak.

Let's say you quote Generic Co.'s CEO at the start of a press release:

> "For years, our users have demanded flip-flops that they can't lose," says Jane Kim, CEO of Generic Co. "That's why we're happy to announce our new line of No-Lose Flip-Flops."

Great! Now quote her again in the last line.

> "Thank you, users," says Jane Kim. "You told us you wanted no-lose flip-flops, and today you can buy them at your local beach store."

Notice that it's not an exact repeat; Jane Kim doesn't say again, "For years, our users have demanded flip-flops that they can't lose." But you still return to where it all started — with a quote from this key leader. The reader might not even recall that's how you started the story, but their brain will make the link.

Last lines are often calls to action — which *also* should circle back to the steak. For instance, if the first line of your sales email is:

> You're invited to subscribe to **Toehold**, my weekly email for flip-flop lovers.

... then your call to action should circle back to that:

> If *you're* one of the world's flip-flop lovers, sign up for **Toehold** right here.

$\sim$ Menu $\sim$

NEW YORK STRIP STEAK

Our house special!

With mashed potatoes and asparagus

$40

APPETIZERS

Assorted Olives	$6
House Pickles	$5
Soft Pretzel	$9
With Bavarian mustard	
Garlic Bread	$6
Hummus Platter	$11
Olives, peppers, pita bread	

SOUPS & SALADS

Garden Salad	$12
Spinach Salad	$9
With strawberries and mint	
Chicken Cobb	$10
Kale Caesar	$8
Thai Noodle Salad	$11
Soup du Jour	$5
Clam Chowder	$6

SANDWICHES

Turkey Melt	$12
Grilled Cheese	$9
Add soup for $3	
Nan's Veggie	$8
Italian Stallion	$11
Reuben	$12
Tofu Tacos	$10
Tuna Salad	$9
Cheeseburger & Fries	$10
BLT	$9

ENTRÉES

Grilled Wild Salmon	$26
Soy-ginger dressing, mashed potatoes	
Chicken Pot Pie	$18
Fish & Chips	$21
Halibut or cod, with fries	

To order the New York Strip Steak, contact your server.

Remember our menu from Secret 3? Check out how it looks with the circle of steak added.

First we put the steak at the top, where it's loud and clear. Now we circle back to the steak at the bottom for our call to action, too.

When it's done right, the circle of steak feels like putting the last piece in a jigsaw puzzle. It clicks. Just as when Simba finally comes home as a grown lion, you recall, "Oh yes, this is where we started."

… before he starts eating all his loyal subjects.

Let's Wrap Up

You see, we *did* keep it short. Let's recap the 3 secrets we talked about in this book.

1. 8 letters or less
2. Get rid of the toilet paper
3. Serve the steak first

Stick with these 3 and you'll go a long way. And remember the 6 bonus tricks:

1. Check your first word
2. Hero words go first or last
3. Numbers go first

4. Try the Big Flip
5. Yes, you should cut that
6. Respect the Circle of Steak

When you write, you may find it's best to make 2 rewrite passes: the first to get rid of long words, then the second for cuts, Big Flips, and all the rest. It won't take forever. You'll get better at it as you go.

Let's end with this idea: remember those short-word ad slogans from Secret 1? They work great, right?

Well, you, my friend, are your own ad agency. The best way to sell yourself to your team, your boss, or your next employer is to make yourself easy to read.

Remember the 3 secrets. Use the short words that pop singers and movie titles use. Take off the toilet paper. Serve the steak first (and chop it up into words of 8 letters or less as you do). Your boss the hyena (and all the other hyenas who read your stuff) will thank you.

Just do it, and you'll find that you really are a better writer than you think.

Resources

Bibliography

Buzzanga, Ally. *Most Recognizable Brand Taglines.* Upwave, 2018.

Jabr, Ferris. "The Reading Brain in the Digital Age: The Science of Paper versus Screens." *Scientific American*, April 11, 2013.

Kuperman, Victor, Sascha Schroeder, and Daniil Gnetov. *Word length and frequency effects on text reading are highly similar in 12 alphabetic languages.* 2023.

Hat Tips

The late Susan Shadburne and Will Vinton gave me my first shot in the film business, and I wouldn't have become a writer without their trust in me. I salute them.

Thanks to all the clients in the 1990s who took a chance on me, and to everyone at Google for sending so much work my way since my first days there in 2004. A special thanks to Masha Fisch, former CMO of Google Analytics, who was the first to suggest I do a writing workshop. That put me on the long road to this book.

My wife, Julie Corwin, has spent a lot of time hearing me yak about these ideas, often in cars or on random city streets. Thank you! Jim Lecinski, Gokul Rajaram, and Michael Foroobar read early drafts of this book and gave me valuable notes.

Special thanks to the terrific team at How2Conquer: Michelle Newcome, Lauren Kelliher, Charlotte Bleau, Telia Garner, and Emily M. Owens — and thanks to old pal Laura Bergheim for hooking us up.

About the Author

FRITZ HOLZNAGEL has spent three decades writing for high-tech firms like Google, for sexy start-ups and sturdy old banks, for the *Dictionary of American History*, and even for *Where in the USA is Carmen Sandiego?* He won an Emmy as a writer of CBS's *A Claymation Easter* and is the author of *Secrets of the Buzzer* and *The Ultimate Droodles Compendium.* He is also the winner of the 1995 *Jeopardy! Tournament of Champions.*

A product of Oregon's fresh air and ocean breezes, Fritz graduated from Willamette University with a degree in history. He now lives near Boston with his wife, Julie, and a yard full of wild rabbits.

Thanks …
And a Big Ask

Thank you so much for reading *8 Letters or Less*. If you enjoyed this book, could you take a moment to give it the boost that only you can deliver?

Share Your Thoughts

Amazon reviews matter — a lot! Here's how you can write one for *8 Letters or Less*:

1. **Log in to your Amazon account:** You'll need to be logged in to leave a review.

2. **Visit the Amazon product page:** Search for *8 Letters or Less* on **amazon.com**.

3. **Click on 'Write a Customer Review':** Scroll down to the Customer Reviews section of the book's page. You'll find a button that says 'Write a customer review.' Click it.

4. **Rate the book:** Choose a star rating that reflects your overall opinion of *8 Letters or Less*. Then …

5. **Write your review:** Share your thoughts on what you liked about the book and how it will help you. Your review doesn't have to be long — just genuine and helpful for future readers.

6. **Submit your review:** Once you're happy with your review, click 'Submit.' Your review will then become part of the book's Amazon page.

Get in Touch

Reach out to me if you'd like to have me come talk to your team.

Email: **fritz@fritzify.com**

LinkedIn: **Fritz Holznagel**

Website: **www.fritzify.com**

Bluesky: **8lettersorless.bsky.social**